# The Activist Manifesto
## by Rupert Younger and Frank Partnoy
## March 2018

**Written**: Late 2017
**First Published**: March 2018
**Source**: www.activistmanifesto.org
**Publisher**:  CreateSpace Independent Publishing Platform

Ta

CW01498104

# Editorial Introduction

Alan D. Morrison
Professor of Law and Finance, Saïd Business School
University of Oxford

In 1837, an interest rate rise in England precipitated a financial panic in the United States. A speculative cotton price bubble burst, there were widespread bank failures, and many states defaulted on their bonds. Trust in bankers plumbed new depths. George Peabody was blackballed by the Reform Club because he was a citizen of a nation that did not pay its debts. The following recession lasted for most of the succeeding decade. And, at the end of that decade, two Prussian intellectuals living in Brussels published a pamphlet whose reverberations we still feel in our intellectual and social life more than a century and a half later.

The Communist Manifesto was written in under two months. When it was published, in February 1848, Karl Marx was 29 years old and his friend Friedrich Engels was 28. They wrote at a time of massive social upheaval: 1848 saw a "Spring of Revolutions," with uprisings in France, Germany, Denmark, the Habsburg Empire, Sweden, Poland and Ireland. None of these revolutions can be attributed to the Manifesto, but its authors appear to have captured something of the spirit of their times; later uprisings have, of course, been more closely associated with the 1848 pamphlet.

It is now eleven years since problems in the US subprime mortgage market triggered a global financial crisis. That crisis saw numerous bank failures and the resultant recession lasted for most of the following decade. Sovereign borrowers in Europe experienced a crisis whose fiscal and social consequences will be felt for decades. And, of course, trust in bankers has plumbed new depths. Fred Goodwin, Chief Executive of the Royal Bank of Scotland from 2001 to 2009, lost his knighthood in 2012.

The years since the financial crisis have seen numerous revolutions. The Arab Spring of 2010—2012 was a wave of demonstrations, protests, and coups in Tunisia, Libya, Egypt, Yemen, Syria and elsewhere. The Occupy Movement has pitched tents in New York, London, and in cities around the world. In June 2016 almost 52% of the British public voted to leave the European Union; in November of the same year, Donald J. Trump was elected 45th President of the United States with 279 electoral college votes. The socialist Bernie Saunders was an important presence throughout the presidential race. Even in the corporate world, traditional governance models are under fire from activist investors: the CEO of Blackrock recently impressed upon business leaders the importance of social contributions that go beyond the generation of profits.

Like the inhabitants of mid-nineteenth century Europe, then, we live in the wake of a calamitous financial crisis and in the midst of whirlwind social change, a popular distaste of financial capitalists, and widespread revolutionary activity. We could use a coherent explanation of the forces that buffet us, and a hint as to their likely resolution. The Victorians had Marx and Engels; we have Rupert Younger and Frank Partnoy. Younger identifies himself with the lower-middle-class Marx, at least in his early poetic Hegelian incarnation, while Partnoy feels an affinity with the wealthy party animal and fox-hunter Engels. Neither Younger nor Partnoy has a beard.

Younger and Partnoy's Activist Manifesto closely follows the format of the 1848 Communist Manifesto, to the extent that the two have a lot of common text. Indeed, anyone familiar with the earlier pamphlet will have to read Younger and Partnoy very carefully to spot the minor textual changes that have a substantial effect upon their meaning.

In light of the close similarity between the two manifestos, the easiest way to interpret Younger and Partnoy's work may be to start from an understanding of the Communist Manifesto. I present below a rapid, and also contestable and personal, summary of its argument.

The Communist Manifesto was commissioned by the Communist League, the first party to espouse the position that would later be characterised as "Marxist." The Manifesto laid out the bare bones of the Marxist position, and it distinguished the Communist League from other parties with similar views. Its first section, "Bourgeois and Proletarians," discusses the class system, famously claiming that "[t]he history of all hitherto existing society is the history of class struggles." What distinguishes the Communist Manifesto is its emphasis upon the technological determinants of that struggle. Marx and Engels claim that the technologies used in production establish the contours of the social classes. In particular, as markets expand and economies of scale become increasingly important, the people who control productive capital become increasingly powerful. Those people are the bourgeoisie, who are "the product of a long course of development, of a series of revolutions in the modes of production and technology."

The ability to service a huge and growing marketplace gives the bourgeoisie enormous social power. They wrest that power from the old feudal landlords, and from the small shop keepers, neither of whom is able to compete in the new capital-intensive marketplace. The acquisition of bourgeois power is accompanied by what Schumpeter would later, in a rather different context, call creative destruction: "[a]ll old-established national industries have been destroyed or are daily being destroyed." Indeed, as this quote suggests, the bourgeoisie's activities transcend the nation state.

The capital controlled by the bourgeoisie requires human labour. That labour is provided by the proletariat. In the long run, anyone who is not a member of the bourgeoisie will either become a member of the proletariat or will drop out of mainstream society (and so will join the lumpenproletariat, "that passively rotting mass thrown off by the lowest layers of the old society"). And, over time, the smaller members of the bourgeoisie will be absorbed by the proletariat, so that capital and social power will become concentrated in a smaller and smaller number of hands. In the struggle to survive, the bourgeoisie compete by "constantly revolutionising the instruments of production," so as to produce more and more. The consequence is periodic crises, caused by over-production, leading to hardship and to a thinning out of the ranks of the bourgeoisie. Ultimately, the whole system must fail, brought down under the weight of its own contradictions.

Marx and Engels identify the important role of the proletariat in precipitating the end of bourgeois capitalism. The proletariat are dis-empowered under the capitalists. They work at the pleasure of the capitalists for subsistence wages, and they are alienated from their own humanity by the division of labour and by the factory system. The system cannot change until the proletariat become aware of their shared interests, and of their capacity to re-capture their humanity by changing society: that is, to employ a phrase that does not appear in the Manifesto, change will occur when the proletariat develop class consciousness. Class consciousness will emerge as the proletariat gather together, and when they become better able to communicate with one another. Both of these criteria are increasingly satisfied as capitalism develops: the massed proletariat in large factories can easily see their common plight, and modern industry creates "improved means of communication." Hence, as capitalism develops, it creates class consciousness and so sows the seeds of its own destruction.

The second section of the Communist Manifesto, "Proletarians and Communists," explains how the Communist League's activities relate to the materialist progression identified in the first section. By Marx and Engels' account, the proletariat have common class interests, if they could only appreciate them. It is therefore logically possible to represent those common interests, and this is what the communists claim to do. They will advance proletarian interests by abolishing bourgeois property, which is a contingent feature of the capitalist society and not an eternal and necessary fact. That abolition will change other contingent features of society: for example, the Manifesto anticipates elements of a feminism that will not properly emerge for another century by arguing (or at least implying) that capitalist power structures render wives a form of property for the male bourgeoisie. Hence, claim Marx and Engels, capitalism engenders "prostitution, both public and private." Capitalism also supports the exploitation of nation by nation, but, because "[t]he working men have no country," and because workers everywhere have a common interest in preventing the exploitation to which they are subject, communists are happy to abolish nationality: communism is international.

This is heady stuff, but it is hardly a programme of action. Marx and Engels provide one towards the end of the second section of the Manifesto. It comprises ten demands that include measures that are now viewed as commonsensical ("free education for all children in public schools. Abolition of children's factory labour in its present form"), that are familiar from many European social democratic programmes ("a heavy progressive or graduated income tax"), that appear in hard-left manifestos ("abolition of all right of inheritance") and hard-right manifestos ("confiscation of the property of all emigrants and rebels"), and that are frankly fantastic ("equal liability of all to labour. Establishment of industrial armies, especially for agriculture"). All of them appear consistent with the central thesis that bourgeois modes of production, and the power relations that go with them, must be phased out. And almost all of them appeared in political manifestos in the century-and-a-half after 1848 publication of the Manifesto.

Section III of the Manifesto contrasts the communists with other socialist movements, all of which it dismisses. Marx and Engels identify three types of socialists. A first group of reactionary socialists opposes the bourgeoisie because it wishes to restore the pre-industrial class system. A second group of conservative socialists hopes, by improving the material conditions of the working poor, to maintain the status quo; this will avert for a while the collapse of the capitalist system, the abolition of bourgeois property, and the dismantling of the bourgeois family and the nation state. A third group of utopian socialists promulgate fantastic systems of social design that, because they pre-empt the emergence of proletariat class consciousness, are unworkable.

The Communist Manifesto concludes by outlining contemporary radical parties and with the famous claim that "[t]he proletarians have nothing to lose but their chains. They have a world to win."

The Communist Manifesto is much-debated and is hard-to-interpret. The Activist Manifesto uses the same structure to make rather different claims. This makes the

Activist Manifesto a very entertaining read, but it also renders it even harder-to-interpret than the Communist Manifesto. The remainder of this Introduction attempts a brief summary of its main points, and provides some suggestion as to their interpretation.

The Activist Manifesto was not commissioned but, had it been, the commission would have come from the Activist League. Younger and Partnoy discuss the role of Activists as a vehicle for social change that mirrors the corresponding role that Marx and Engels identify for communists and, indeed, Younger and Partnoy reproduce a lot of the Communist Manifesto's text. But, while Marx and Engels are concerned with the historic development of the proletariat and its interests, Younger and Partnoy write about a class of Have-Nots, who are engaged in a struggle with the Haves. Indeed, with the exception of a passing reference to the lumpenhavenots that is included for literary reasons, Younger and Partnoy mention no other social classes.

The organisation of the Activist Manifesto mirrors that of the Communist Manifesto. Section I presents a materialist conception of the Haves and the Have-Nots, whose struggles comprise the history of all hitherto existing society. Section II introduces the activists and relates them to the interests of the Have-Nots; like Section II of the Communist Manifesto, the Activist Manifesto here includes a list of immediate measures to be taken by the activists. Section III discusses the relationship between the activists, as conceived by Younger and Partnoy, and other groups that claim to represent the interests of the Have-Nots. Section IV concludes: like the proletariat, the Have-Nots have nothing to lose but their chains, and they have a world to win.

While the two Manifestos share a good deal of text, they differ in significant ways. Section I of the Communist Manifesto adumbrates a materialist account of society that claims to highlight inherent contradictions whose resolution must eventually change property rights, the institutions of the family, and the nation state in profound ways. By my reading, the Activist Manifesto does not make such strong claims. To be sure, it lays a variety of sins at the feet of the Haves. They exploit the Have-Nots in their own generation and, through their abuse of the environment, those of future generations. They undermine the political process by making the absurd assertion that corporate political expenditure is a form of protected free speech. Like the bourgeoisie of 1848, the Haves appropriate new technologies and so as better to exploit the Have-Nots. They also over-produce, creating "too many extravagant properties and toys." Marx and Engels note that the bourgeoisie strip "the physician, the lawyer, the priest, the poet, the man of science" of the "reverent awe" that they were once afforded; Younger and Partnoy add to this list of hitherto honoured professions that of "IT consultant," who, in 2018, are denied any reverence at all, and, like the others, are "mere wage labourers."

Marx and Engels can see some good in the bourgeois revolution, and Younger and Partnoy are similarly willing to acknowledge worth in the actions of the Haves. Both the bourgeois and the Haves have rendered "[n]ational one-sidedness and narrow-mindedness [...] more and more impossible." The Haves and the bourgeoisie have both "created more massive and more colossal productive forces than have all preceding generations together." But, while Marx and Engels celebrate our rescue by the bourgeois "from the idiocy of rural life," Younger and Partnoy claim that the Haves have "created permanent economic and social ghettos of the countryside and the rural towns."

But the implications of Haves behaviour in 2018 appears different to that of bourgeois hegemony in 1848. Marx and Engels believed that, as a proletariat class consciousness emerged, capitalism would collapse under the weight of its contradictions. Younger and Partnoy appear, rather, to believe that the Have-Nots will be able to ensure that the system works for them without going so far as completely to destroy it. Hence, while their access to Twitter, Facebook, and other social media enables the type of Have-Not coordination that the Communist Manifesto predicts for the proletariat in the final stages of capitalism, Younger and Partnoy do not believe that the consequence will be a total revolution; that the "Haves are unfit any longer to be the ruling class in society" does not mean that the basic institutions of society must be overthrown; rather, it means that members of the Have-Nots should ultimately assume a more important role.

That Younger and Partnoy subscribe to this evolutionary view of society is clearer from Section II of the Activist Manifesto than it is from Section I. In Section II, Younger and Partnoy explicitly contrast the communist belief that property is a bourgeois institution that cannot outlive the bourgeois with their own position that activists should "provide security and protect private property, including intellectual property."

If Younger and Partnoy's activists do not aim for the abolition of bourgeois property, then the power systems that it reflects will presumably also survive the onslaught of the activists; those systems will simply provide a better deal for the Have-Nots. Are Younger and Partnoy simply promulgating the sort of conservative socialism excoriated in Section III of the Communist Manifesto?

Younger and Partnoy are prevented by the straightjacket of the Manifesto format from addressing this question head-on. We can get some traction on it by considering two questions. First, precisely who are the Haves and the Have-Nots? Second, what do the Activists really stand for?

The natural answer to the first question would appear to be that Haves own a lot more stuff than Have-Nots. But a system that retains the social institution of property in its current form will inevitably exhibit material inequality. A careful reading of Section II of the Activist Manifesto indicates that, in fact, Younger and Partnoy's Have-Nots are those who are dispossessed of power. A similar observation could be made of the proletarians in the Communist Manifesto, of course. But in the 1848 Manifesto, the distribution of power is governed by the distribution of capital and, hence, reflects productive relations in society. Section II of the 2018 Manifesto avoids reference to capital in this context: it focuses directly upon the distribution of power in a property-owning society. If power can be returned from the Haves to the Have-Nots, then it can be done so without the abolition of property.

Of course, if one is possessed of property, then one has powers denied to someone who lacks possessions. But one should not be denied the respect that is due to any person: that is, one should have the power to form opinions and to be heard on an equal footing with others. One should have the power to form moral judgements, and to act upon them without fear of retribution from others, whether they have property or not. I believe that, if we interpret "power" in this way as the possession of the rights to deliberate, to be heard, and to act, then one can characterise the Haves and the Have-Nots of Younger and Partnoy's Manifesto as being those who have, and those who have not, this type of power. Section I of the Activist Manifesto indicates that the Haves attempt to retain their monopoly on this type of respect by denying it wherever possible to the Have-Nots.

Hence, for example, Younger and Partnoy argue that abolition of property cannot on its own resolve the Have-Nots problems, because it could "be co-opted by the Haves for their own benefit." Younger and Partnoy do not expand upon this point. But I think it means that, in a system within which some people (the Haves) are able to restrict the moral agency of others (the Have-Nots), abolition of property will simply involve greater restriction of the Have-Nots' agency: as the Bonzo Dog Doo Da Band have it, "No matter who you vote for, the government always gets in." More prosaically, Younger and Partnoy appear, as I do, to subscribe to the position that a well-structured system of property rights protects the personal space and the moral agency of the unpowerful. Centralised state power is unlikely to accomplish either goal: Younger and Partnoy cleverly make this point by inserting the word "not" into Marx and Engels's statement that the proletariat (the Haves in the 2018 document) will wrest power to centralise production in the hands of the state.

We can attempt to interpret the Younger and Partnoy version of activism in light of this vision of the Have/Have-Not divide. Activists should attempt to protect the freedom to reason, the right to be heard, and the moral agency of the dispossessed Have-Nots. This, at least, is how I wish to interpret Younger and Partnoy's statement that activists should "[f]ight inequality and vested interests." By my account, a vested interest is a lobby with the power to suppress the ability to reason (for example, by misleading the Have-Nots), to deny people the right to be heard respectfully (for example by misrepresenting or dismissing their views in the print media), or to prevent people from exercising moral agency (for example, by compelling them to mis-sell retail financial products against the threat of job loss).

This interpretation resolves a problem raised by a casual reading of Younger and Partnoy. If the Have-Nots were simply those with few material possessions, or those with less social power, than the Haves, then it is not clear why we should view the Have-Nots as speaking with one voice. And yet Younger and Partnoy follow Marx and Engels in their claim that the Have-Nots have a collective interest. That collective interest emerges in the Communist Manifesto because the proletarians have a common interest in the abolition of the bourgeois system of production that alienates and suppresses them. But, as I have already noted, the Have-Nots have no natural interest in revolution, nor in the abolition of property, religion, or the family. It is perfectly feasible that one class of Have-Nots may be antagonistic towards another: the recent history of the Middle East appears to support this conclusion as, for that matter, did the 2016 US presidential race. Giving way to this type of antagonism is wrong insofar as it denies others the rights to reason, to be heard, and to act: if one Have-Not believes that he ought to deny another those rights, then he suffers from a sort of Younger and Partnoy version of "false consciousness" that relates to our shared humanity rather than, in the Marxian sense, to our shared class interests.

Section II of Younger and Partnoy's Manifesto follows the 1848 pamphlet by enumerating ten measures that the activists will enact. All seem completely reasonable to a liberal member of the bourgeois such as myself. Younger and Partnoy call for minimum standards of living, for a respect for the environment, for diversity, and for affordable health care. They support education and something that they refer to as "knowledge creation." They wish to protect private property, to ensure that the financial sector enables economic growth, and to decentralise power. They want to improve internet access, and they aim to "root out and pursue corruption and the entrenchment of power, both in government and in the private sector." All of these measures can be viewed as steps along the path towards a society in which all have a meaningful voice. In a longer document, Younger and Partnoy would surely have expanded upon the relationship of each measure to the ultimate goal of the activists.

Like Marx and Engels, Younger and Partnoy devote Section III of their Manifesto to a discussion of ill-conceived and false activism. For example, they dismiss financial activism as "profoundly selfish," arguing that it "lacks a social or moral compass." Doubtless this is frequently true. But financial activists form a view, express an opinion, and attempt to act upon it. They are at least due the respect that any other person is due in attempting to exercise his or her agency. A longer discussion of the faults in financial activism would be helpful: are Younger and Partnoy concerned that financial activists attempt to suppress the agency of workers, or of trades unionists, for example?

One could deploy the same response to Younger and Partnoy's statement that environmentalism "is both reactionary and Utopian," although I must admit to enjoying their conclusion that the last words of environmentalism are "the Roundtable for Sustainable Palm Oil, Swampy, Earth Day, Greenham Common, and composting." And, while Younger and Partnoy believe that community activist concerns over speeding motorbikes, fly-tippers and dangerous playgrounds are "as noble as the grand aims and ambitions of those who seek to change a country or the planet," they also worry that local activists simply impose externalities upon other communities. Are local activists acting on their moral reasoning, or are they denying the moral agency of their neighbours? Younger and Partnoy appear to draw the latter conclusion; I favour the former. And I have a similar concern with respect to Younger and Partnoy's criticism of the Occupy movement's utopianism. In the Communist Manifesto, that utopianism is an attempt to design a proletarian society before history has advanced sufficiently far to accommodate it; but, by my reading of the 2018 Manifesto, we should not wait for history to ripen before affording people the power and respect to which they are due. What, then, is morally wrong with a utopian position, however misguided one may believe it to be?

The Activist Manifesto is both great fun and also a timely call to action. Large minorities of national populations all over the developed world feel ignored and voiceless. They believe that they are denied the information they need to make informed choices and to act morally. They are the Have-Nots. Have-Nots believe that they are not being accorded the basic respect that is due to them and, of late, they have expressed their frustration at the ballot box and elsewhere. A Have who expresses her belief that Have-Not behaviour is irrational, misguided and stupid merely compounds the problem by denying the Have-Nots the respectful hearing that is due to them. What the Have-Nots need is activism. Younger and Partnoy provide a brief blueprint that may help us to provide it.

The Russian Revolution erupted sixty-nine years after the publication of the Communist Manifesto, and it shaped our politics and our public discourse for the rest of the twentieth century. Marx, of course, felt that the first time that history repeats itself, it does so as tragedy. An activist revolution would not, however, be a tragedy. It would be an opportunity to repair some of the deepest fractures in our current polity. One can only hope that we do not have to wait until 2087[1] to witness it.

*Oxford, March 2018*

---

1 Let CT be the date on which the Communist Manifesto was published, AT be the publication date for the Activist Manifesto and RR be the date of the Russian Revolution. Then 2087 = AT + (RR-CT).

# Preface to the 2018 Edition

## Rupert Younger & Frank Partnoy

This pamphlet is an imagining of what Karl Marx and Friedrich Engels would write today – 170 years after publication of *The Communist Manifesto*. We stumbled onto this idea after nearly a decade of conversations about activism, not only in politics – where, as we write here, **"Activists have threatened the established world order, in Tunisia and Egypt and Syria and Indonesia, in defeating Hillary Clinton, in the Brexit vote, and in elections throughout the world"** – but also in the markets and in society more generally.

Our main expertise has been in shareholder activism, where we have advised many of the largest hedge funds and have published leading academic studies. But as the two of us discussed activism conceptually over the years, we imagined what might happen if shareholder activists joined with political and social activists as a united front.

We speculated that pensioners might join with hedge funds and community activists to press a company for social change. We didn't imagine specifically that the massive pension fund for California teachers would partner with a multi-billion dollar hedge fund to push Apple to reform the way children interact with their phones (as is happening now), but that kind of union was what we have had in mind: activists of various types emerging from their separate silos to advocate for change together.

On 13th April, 2017, we were having a wide-ranging telephone conversation about our ideas, and Frank (who plays the role of Engels in our story) asked Rupert (Marx) the following radical question: "What do you think Marx and Engels would say about the various financial, political, and social movements today?" (Engels was the more empirically-minded of the two, while Marx was more of a poet-philosopher.)

While Rupert was laughing at the seemingly preposterous idea, Frank downloaded a copy of *The Communist Manifesto*, copied its text into a shared Google docs file, and the two of us began reading aloud. What we saw on the page, in our new reimagined context, took our breath away. The *Manifesto* spoke to us directly and germanely, as if Marx and Engels had anticipated the revolutionary movements of the twenty-first century. The words were surprisingly resonant, even though neither of us had been particularly sympathetic to communist economics or philosophy.

As we read through the document, we saw many paragraphs that needed an updating. Some notions were no longer relevant, or had been proved wrong. But still, the document had bones. It just needed a few tweaks and tucks. We quickly edited and supplemented the famous first paragraph:

> **"A spectre is haunting Europe – the spectre of communism. All the powers of old Europe have entered into a holy alliance to exorcise this spectre: Pope and Tsar, Metternich and Guizot, French Radicals and German police-spies."**

So that it became:

"A spectre is haunting the world – the spectre of activism. All the powers of the old world order have entered into a holy alliance to exorcise this spectre: the corporate Haves, the elites, the billionaires, the establishment politicians of the Republican and Democratic Parties, Conservatives and Labour, the talking heads at Davos, the echo chambers of online media and fake news."

And then we continued during the next weeks and months, word by word, keeping the text where it still sang, but repairing and reconstructing, just as we would renovate an old house. We cut out many of their specific proposals, which needed to be modernized. But the vast majority of their language – 74 percent of the original words – remained intact.

We felt justified in our renovation based on Marx and Engels's own reflections from 1872, twenty-five years after they first began the discussions following the First Congress of the Communist League. They wrote:

"The practical application of the principles will depend, as the Manifesto itself states, everywhere and at all times, on the historical conditions for the time being existing, and, for that reason, no special stress is laid on the revolutionary measures proposed at the end of Section II."

We agree. Historical conditions have changed. The world is in need of new revolutionary measures, the ones we believe Marx and Engels would have advocated if they were alive today.

This is their new manifesto. *The Activist Manifesto.*

# Manifesto of the Activist Party

A spectre is haunting the world – the spectre of activism. All the powers of the world order have entered into a holy alliance to exorcise this spectre: the corporate Haves, the elites, the billionaires, the establishment politicians of the Republican and Democratic Parties, Conservatives and Labour, the talking heads at Davos, the echo chambers of online media and fake news.

Activists have threatened this established order, in Tunisia and Egypt and Syria and Indonesia, in defeating Hillary Clinton, in the Brexit vote, and in elections throughout the world. Activists have threatened the powers of corporate managers, of those who would destroy the environment or oppress the powerless. But activism also has been co-opted and thwarted in turn, by rulers who lure activists for votes but then pursue narrow self-interest. Activists work in silos, and stay in silos, until they are appropriated by the very powers they enable, are denigrated as special interests, or are simply ignored.

Where is the party in opposition that has not been decried as activist by its opponents in power? Where is the opposition that has not hurled back the branding reproach of activism, against the more advanced opposition parties, as well as against its reactionary adversaries?

Two things result from this fact:

I. Activism is already acknowledged by all global powers to be itself a power.

II. It is high time that Activists should openly, in the face of the whole world, publish their views, their aims, their tendencies, and meet this nursery tale of the Spectre of Activism with a manifesto of an Activist Party itself.

To this end, we call on Activists in their fields, working in their particular silos, to gather together to initiate a new global movement of change. We put forth a manifesto to unlock the power of Activists all over the world to mount a unified challenge against the globally entrenched group of Haves whose power and single-minded self-preservation strategy is one of divide and rule.

Only by working together can the Have-Nots realize the true power of Activism.

# I. Haves and Have-Nots

The history of all hitherto existing society is the history of struggles between those who Have, and those who Have-Not.

Freeman and slave, patrician and plebeian, lord and serf, guild-master and journeyman – in simple terms, Haves and Have-Nots – have stood in constant opposition to one another, carried on an uninterrupted, now hidden, now open fight, a fight that each time ended, either in a revolutionary reconstitution of society at large, or in the common ruin of the contending groups.

In the earlier epochs of history, we find almost everywhere a complicated arrangement of society into various orders, a manifold gradation of social and economic rank ranging from the Haves at the top of the order to the Have-Nots at the bottom. In Ancient Rome we have patricians, knights, plebeians, slaves; in the Middle Ages, feudal lords, vassals, guild-masters, journeymen, apprentices, serfs; in the Modern Capitalist Era, we have billionaires, political and economic elites, salaried workers, casual workers, the unemployed and the unemployable: in almost all of these groups, again, subordinate gradations.

From the serfs of the Middle Ages sprang the chartered burghers of the earliest towns. From these burgesses the first elements of the Haves were developed. The growth of international trade in the seventeenth and eighteenth centuries established the commercial structures essential to the success of the Haves. The industrialisation of the nineteenth century supercharged the returns available from these structures and the technological boom of the twentieth century further cemented the hold of the Haves on the top tiers of the establishment economic, social, and political hierarchy.

Before 1848, many different socialist enclaves around the world advocated a more idealized and fair society. A spectre of a different kind then blocked their collective action, and the Haves appropriated the Have-Nots message until they united to threaten the establishment.

By the start of our twenty-first century, we are faced with the extraordinary fact that the top one percent of the world's population own the same resources as the remaining ninety-nine percent. Those at the bottom are less upwardly mobile than in previous generations; entrance to wealthy gated communities is blocked, not only by private security forces, but also by the increasingly prohibitive costs of health care, technology, and education. There is the dominant force of mass incarceration, with millions of poor, minorities, and powerless walled off from the rulers they might threaten. The Haves have never in history held so much advantage over the Have-Nots.

As with the manias, panics, and crashes of history, the dislocations arising from the financial crisis created new opportunities for the Haves to benefit from seizing the political response. The use and abuse of complex financial innovation – derivatives, structured products, credit default swaps, and collateralized debt obligations – have extended the financial system beyond its primary purpose of facilitating economic growth and matching borrowers and savers to secondary and more dubious purposes.

Organisations, financed by this welter of complex money and in thrall to the ideal of delivering profit above all else, have laid waste to the natural resources of the very ground they inhabit. Unbelievers in the ideal of inter-generational responsibility, their single pursuit is the betterment of themselves in their own time, entrenching their Have status at the expense not only of today's Have-Nots but also generations of Have-Nots to come. Foremost in our epoch is the destruction of our physical environs, with the melting of polar icecaps and widespread climate change exerting pressure on living creatures everywhere. The externalization of environmental costs to future generations enables the profligate lifestyle of the Haves.

Beyond the environment is the rise of the newest form of social inequality. Despite the huge progress made by previous generations of activists seeking social progress, our epoch is host to one of the greatest splits in social strata that the world has ever seen. The world's eight richest people – billionaires worth over $425bn – collectively have as much wealth as the poorest 3.6 billion people, half of the planet.

The Haves assert that political expenditures are protected speech. They form and endow foundations to harness and co-opt the productive young minds and assets in pursuit of their favoured agendas. A wave of new laws and regulations come to depend on narrow agendas instead of broad ideals. The once-laudable protection of private property becomes the dubious exploitation of intellectual property and monopoly rents. The Haves misappropriate not only economic power, but also political, social, and charitable power. Thus, the modern Haves are the product of technology, financial innovation, and political capture.

In today's epoch, this split between the Haves and the Have-Nots has become a rupture. Democracy and transparency could have been great equalisers. Commerce and technology could have been great levellers. Instead, all of these forces have been co-opted by the Haves and, instead of a great society, our epoch has produced two hostile camps, the Haves and Have-Nots, facing each other across a rift of inequality.

The Haves, historically, have played a most revolutionary part.

The Haves, wherever they have got the upper hand, have put an end to all feudal, patriarchal, idyllic relations. They have pitilessly torn asunder the motley feudal ties that bound humans to their "natural superiors", and have left remaining no other nexus between person and person than naked self- interest, than callous "cash payment". They have drowned the most heavenly ecstasies of religious fervour, of chivalrous enthusiasm, of philistine sentimentalism, in the icy water of egotistical calculation. They have resolved personal worth into exchange value, and in place of the numberless indefeasible chartered freedoms, have set up that single, unconscionable freedom – Free Trade. In one word, for exploitation, veiled by religious and political illusions, they have substituted naked, shameless, direct, brutal exploitation.

The Haves have stripped of their halo every occupation hitherto honoured and looked up to with reverent awe. They have converted the physician, the lawyer, the priest, the poet, the scientist, the IT consultant, into mere wage labourers, while the fruits of the technological revolution are enjoyed by a fortunate few.

The Haves have torn away from the family its sentimental veil, and have reduced the family relation to a mere money relation.

The Haves have disclosed how it came to pass that the brutal display of vigour in the Middle Ages, which reactionaries so much admire, found its fitting complement in the most slothful indolence. They have been the first to show what human activity can bring about. It has accomplished wonders far surpassing Egyptian pyramids, Roman aqueducts, and Gothic cathedrals; it has conducted expeditions that put in the shade all former Exoduses of nations and crusades. It has connected nations and people, and enabled humans to hold the world's information in the palm of their hands.

The Haves cannot exist without constantly revolutionising the instruments of production and finance, and thereby the relations of production and finance, and with them the whole relations of society. Conservation of the old modes of production in unaltered form was, on the contrary, the first condition of existence for all earlier industrial classes. Constant revolutionising of production, uninterrupted disturbance of all social conditions, everlasting uncertainty and agitation distinguish this Haves epoch from all earlier ones. All fixed, fast-frozen relations, with their train of ancient and venerable prejudices and opinions, are swept away, all new-formed ones become antiquated before they can ossify. Data become bits, words become waves, ideas are shot throughout the planet in an instant. All that is solid melts into air, all that is holy is profaned, and humans are at last compelled to face with sober senses their real conditions of life, and their relations with their kind.

The need of a constantly expanding market for their products chases the Haves over the entire surface of the globe. They must nestle everywhere, settle everywhere, establish connexions everywhere.

The Haves have through their exploitation of the world market given a cosmopolitan character to production and consumption in every country. To the great chagrin of isolationists and protectionists, they have drawn from under the feet of industry the national ground on which they stood. All old-established national industries have been destroyed or are daily being destroyed. They are dislodged by new industries, whose introduction becomes a life and death question for all civilised nations, by industries that no longer work up indigenous raw material, but raw material drawn from the remotest zones; industries whose products are consumed, not only at home, but in every quarter of the globe. In place of the old wants, satisfied by the production of the country, we find new wants, requiring for their satisfaction the products of distant lands and climes. In place of the old local and national seclusion and self-sufficiency, we have intercourse in every direction, universal inter-dependence of nations. And as in material, so also in intellectual production. The intellectual creations of individual nations become common property. National one-sidedness and narrow-mindedness become more and more impossible, and from the numerous national and local literatures, there arises a world literature.

The Haves, by the rapid improvement of all instruments of production, by the immensely facilitated means of communication, draw all, even the most barbarian, nations into civilisation. The cheap prices of commodities are the heavy artillery with which they batter down all Chinese walls, with which they force the barbarians' intensely obstinate hatred of foreigners to capitulate. They compel all nations, on pain of extinction, to adopt the Haves' mode of production; they compel them to introduce what they call civilisation into their midst, i.e., to become Haves themselves. In one word, they create a world after their own image.

The Haves have subjected the world to the rule of the elites. They have created enormous cities, have greatly increased the urban population as compared with the rural, and have thus created permanent economic and social ghettos of the countryside and the rural towns. Just as they have made much of the country dependent on cities, so they continue to make third world and second world countries dependent on first world ones, the nations of Haves.

The modern Haves, during their rule of less than two hundred years, have created more massive and more colossal productive forces than have all preceding generations together. Subjection of Nature's forces, technology, the application of science to industry and agriculture, global travel, instant communication, the mass appropriation of whole continents, the oceans and even space – what earlier century had even a presentiment that such productive forces slumbered in the lap of social labour?

We see then: the means of production and of exchange, on whose foundation the Haves built themselves up, were generated in feudal society. At a certain stage in the development of these means of production and of exchange, the conditions under which feudal society produced and exchanged, the feudal organisation of agriculture and manufacturing industry, in one word, the feudal relations of property became no longer compatible with the already developed productive forces; they became so many fetters. They had to be burst asunder; they were burst asunder.

Into their place stepped free competition, accompanied by a social and political constitution adapted in it, and the economic and political sway of the Haves class.

A similar movement is going on before our own eyes. Modern Capitalist society, with its relations of production and finance, of exchange and of property, a society that has conjured up such gigantic means of production and of exchange, is like the sorcerer who is no longer able to control the powers of the nether world whom he has called up by his spells.

For many a decade past the history of industry and commerce is but the history of the revolt of modern productive forces against modern conditions of production, against the property relations that are the conditions for the existence of the Haves and of their rule. It is enough to mention the commercial crises that by their periodical return put the existence of the entire Haves society on its trial, each time more threateningly.

In these crises, a great part not only of the existing products, but also of the previously created productive forces, are periodically destroyed. In these crises, there breaks out an epidemic that, in all earlier epochs, would have seemed an absurdity – the epidemic of over-production. Society suddenly finds itself put back into a state of momentary barbarism; it appears as if a famine, a universal war of devastation, had cut off the supply of every means of subsistence; industry and commerce seem to be destroyed; and why? Because there is too much civilisation, too much means of subsistence, too much industry, too much commerce, too many extravagant properties and toys. The productive forces at the disposal of society no longer tend to further the development of the conditions of property owned by the Haves; on the contrary, they have become too powerful for these conditions, by which they are fettered, and so soon as they overcome these fetters, they bring disorder into the whole of Haves society, endanger the existence of the Haves' property. The conditions of Haves society are too narrow to comprise the wealth created by them.

And how do the Haves get over these crises? On the one hand by enforced destruction of a mass of productive forces; on the other, by the conquest of new markets, and by the more thorough exploitation of the old ones. That is to say, by paving the way for more extensive and more destructive crises, and by diminishing the means whereby crises are prevented.

The weapons with which the Haves felled feudalism to the ground are now turned against the Haves themselves.

But not only have the Haves forged the weapons that bring death to themselves; they have also called into existence the men and women who are to wield those weapons – the modern working class – the Have-Nots. These labourers, who must sell themselves piecemeal, are a commodity, like every other article of commerce, and are consequently exposed to all the vicissitudes of competition, to all the fluctuations of the market.

Owing to the extensive use of technology, and to the division of labour, the work of the Have-Nots has lost all individual character, and, consequently, all charm. The Have-Nots become an appendage of the computer or robot, and it is only the most simple, most monotonous, and most easily acquired knack, that is required of them.

Hence, the cost of production of workers is restricted, almost entirely, to the means of subsistence that they require for maintenance, and for the propagation of their race. But the price of a commodity, and therefore also of labour, is equal to its cost of production. In proportion, therefore, as the repulsiveness of the work increases, the wage decreases. Nay more, in proportion as the use of technology increases, in the same proportion the availability of satisfying work disappears. In too many communities, the only available work is at minimum wage, on the street in gangs, or in prison.

Modern Industry has converted the little workshop of the patriarchal master into the great factory of the industrial capitalist. Masses of labourers, crowded into the factory, are organised like soldiers. As privates of the industrial army they are placed under the command of a perfect hierarchy of officers and sergeants. Not only are they slaves of the Haves class, and of the Haves State; they are daily and hourly enslaved by the machine, by the overlooker, outsourced to robots, to the benefit of the individual Haves manufacturers themselves. The more openly this despotism proclaims gain to be its end and aim, the more petty, the more hateful and the more embittering it is.

The less the skill and exertion of strength implied in manual labour, in other words, the more modern industry becomes developed, the more is the labour of men and women superseded by that of automation. Differences of age and sex have no longer any distinctive social validity for the working class. All are instruments of labour, more or less expensive to use, according to their age and sex.

No sooner is the exploitation of the labourer by the manufacturer, so far, at an end, that they receive their wages in cash, than they are set upon by the other portions of the Haves, the landlord, the shopkeeper, the pawnbroker, the pyramid schemer, etc.

The lower strata of the middle class – the small tradespeople, shopkeepers, and fast-food workers, the handicraftsmen and peasants – all these sink gradually into the Have-Nots, partly because their diminutive capital does not suffice for the scale on which Modern Industry is carried on, and is swamped in the competition with the large capitalists, partly because their specialised skill is rendered worthless by new methods of production. Thus the Have-Nots recruited from all classes of the population.

The Have-Nots go through various stages of development. With their birth begins the struggle with the Haves. At first the contest is carried on by individuals, then by small groups, then by the operative of one faction, in one locality, against the individual Have who directly exploits them. They direct their attacks not against the Have conditions of production, but against the instruments of production themselves; they destroy imported wares that compete with their labour, they smash to pieces machinery, they set factories ablaze, they occupy – from Wall Street to Tahrir Square – and they agitate in remote online corners, seeking to build forces to restore by persuasion their vanished status.

At this stage, the Have-Nots still form an incoherent mass scattered over the whole country and world, and broken up by their mutual competition. If anywhere they unite to form more compact bodies, this is not yet the consequence of their own active union, but of the union of the Haves, whose class, in order to attain its own political ends, is compelled to set the whole of the Have-Nots in motion, and is moreover yet, for a time, able to do so. At this stage, therefore, the Have-Nots do not fight their enemies, but the enemies of their enemies, the remnants of absolute monarchy, the landowners, the non-industrial Haves, the petty Haves. Thus, the whole historical movement is concentrated in the hands of the Haves; every victory so obtained is a victory for the Haves.

But with the development of industry, the Have-Nots not only increase in number; they become concentrated in greater masses, their strength grows, and they feel that strength more. The various interests and conditions of life within the ranks of the Have-Nots are more and more equalised, and nearly everywhere the quality of life is reduced to the same low level. The growing competition among the Haves, and the resulting commercial crises, create uncertainty among the Have-Nots. The increasing improvement of technology, ever more rapidly developing, makes their livelihood more and more precarious; social interactions take more and more the character of collisions between two classes. Thereupon, different groups of Have-Nots begin to form combinations against the Haves; they club together in order to keep up their rights against corruption or abuse of power or discrimination based on minority classifications; they found permanent associations in order to make provision beforehand for these occasional revolts. Here and there, the contest breaks out into riots.

Now and then Have-Nots are victorious, but only for a time. The real fruit of their battles lies, not in the immediate result, but in their ever-expanding union. This union is helped on by the improved means of communication that are created by modern industry, Twitter, Facebook, and social media, and that place Have-Nots of different localities in contact with one another. It was just this contact that was needed to centralise the numerous local struggles, all of the same character, into one national struggle between classes. But every class struggle is a political struggle. And that union, to attain which the burghers of the Middle Ages, with their miserable highways, required centuries, the modern Have-Nots, thanks to the Internet, achieve in a few weeks or months.

This organisation of the Have-Nots into a class, and, consequently into a political party, is continually being upset again by the competition between the Have-Not segments themselves. But it ever rises up again, stronger, firmer, mightier. It compels legislative recognition of the particular interests of Have-Nots, by taking advantage of the divisions among the Haves themselves.

Altogether collisions between the classes of the old society further, in many ways, the course of development of the Have-Nots. The Haves find themselves involved in a constant battle. At first with the aristocracy; later on, with those portions of the Haves themselves, whose interests have become antagonistic to the progress of industry; at all time with the Haves of foreign countries. In all these battles, it sees itself compelled to appeal to the Have-Nots, to ask for help, and thus, to drag it into the political arena. The Haves themselves, therefore, supply the Have-Nots with their own elements of political and general education, in other words, they furnish the Have-Nots with weapons for fighting the Haves.

Further, as we have already seen, entire sections of the ruling class are, by the advance of industry, precipitated into the Have-Nots, or are at least threatened in their conditions of existence. These also supply the Have-Nots with fresh elements of enlightenment and progress.

Finally, in times when the class struggle nears the decisive hour, the progress of dissolution going on within the ruling class, in fact within the whole range of old society, assumes such a violent, glaring character, that a small section of the Haves cuts itself adrift, and joins the Have-Nots, the class that holds the future in its hands. Just as, therefore, at an earlier period, a section of the nobility went over to the

Haves, so now a portion of the Haves goes over to the Have-Nots, and in particular, a portion of the Haves who are ideologists, who have raised themselves to the level of comprehending theoretically the historical movement as a whole.

Of all the classes that stand face to face with the Haves today, the Have-Nots alone are a really revolutionary class. The other classes decay and finally disappear in the face of Modern Industry; the Have-Nots are its special and essential product.

The lower middle class, the small manufacturer, the shopkeeper, the artisan, the peasant, the migrant worker, the home health care aide, all these fight against the Haves, to save from extinction their existence as fractions of the middle class. They are therefore not revolutionary, but conservative. Nay more, they are reactionary, for they try to roll back the wheel of history. If by chance, they are revolutionary, they are only so in view of their impending transfer into the Have-Nots; they thus defend not their present, but their future interests, they desert their own standpoint to place themselves at that of the Have-Nots.

The "dangerous class", what might be called *lumpenhavenot*, the social scum, that passively rotting mass thrown off by the lowest layers of the old society, may, here and there, be swept into the movement by a Have-Not revolution; its conditions of life, however, prepare it far more for the part of a bribed tool of reactionary intrigue.

In the condition of the Have-Nots, those of old society at large are already virtually swamped. The Have-Nots are without property; their relation to their partners and children have no longer anything in common with the Haves family relations; modern industry labour, modern subjection to capital, the same in England as in France, in America as in Germany, has stripped them of every trace of national character. Law, morality, religion, are to them so many Haves prejudices, behind which lurk in ambush just as many Haves interests.

All the preceding classes that got the upper hand sought to fortify their already acquired status by subjecting society at large to their conditions of appropriation. The Have-Nots cannot become masters of the productive forces of society, except by abolishing their own previous mode of appropriation, and thereby also every other previous mode of appropriation. They have nothing of their own to secure and to fortify; their mission is to destroy all previous securities for, and insurances of, individual property.

All previous historical movements were movements of minorities, or in the interest of minorities. The Have-Not movement is the self-conscious, independent movement of the immense majority, in the interest of the immense majority. The Have-Nots, the lowest stratum of our present society, cannot stir, cannot raise themselves up, without the whole superincumbent strata of official society being sprung into the air.

Though not in substance, yet in form, the struggle of the Have-Nots with the Haves is at first a national struggle. The Have-Nots of each country must, of course, first of all settle matters with their own Haves.

In depicting the most general phases of the development of the Have-Nots, we traced the more or less veiled civil war, raging within existing society, up to the point where that war breaks out into open revolution, and where the violent overthrow of the Haves lays the foundation for the sway of the Have-Nots.

Hitherto, every form of society has been based, as we have already seen, on the antagonism of oppressing and oppressed classes. But in order to oppress a class, certain conditions must be assured to it under which it can, at least, continue its slavish existence. The serfs, in the period of serfdom, raised themselves to membership in the commune, just as the petty Haves, under the yoke of the feudal absolutism, managed to develop into Haves. The modern labourers, on the contrary, instead of rising with the process of industry, sink deeper and deeper below the conditions of existence of their own class. They become paupers, and pauperism develops more rapidly than population and wealth. And here it becomes evident, that the Haves are unfit any longer to be the ruling class in society, and to impose their conditions of existence upon society as an over-riding law. These Haves are unfit to rule because they are incompetent to assure an existence to its slave within slavery, because they cannot help letting the slaves sink into such a state, that it has to feed them, instead of being fed by them. Society can no longer live under these Haves, in other words, their existence is no longer compatible with society.

The essential conditions for the existence and for the sway of the Haves class is the formation and augmentation of capital; when the rate of return to capital is greater then the rate of return to wage-labour, the gap between Haves and Have-Nots inevitably will widen, as has been the case during the previous century. The advance of industry, whose involuntary promoter is the Haves, thus incentivizes activism, as Have-Nots come to see the potential gains from revolutionary combination, due to association. The development of Modern Industry, therefore, cuts from under its feet the very foundation on which the Haves produce and appropriate products. What the Haves therefore produce, above all, are their own grave-diggers. Their fall and the victory of the Have-Nots are equally inevitable.

# II. Have-Nots and Activists

In what relation do the Activists stand to the Have-Nots as a whole?

The Activists do not form a separate party opposed to other activist parties.

They have no interests separate and apart from those of the Have-Nots as a whole.

They do not set up any sectarian principles of their own, by which to shape and mould a modern Have-Not movement.

The Activists are distinguished from the other activist movements by this only: 1. In the struggles of the Have-Nots, they point out and bring to the front the common interests of the entirety of the Have-Nots, independently of any individual activist's silo interests. 2. In the various stages of development that the struggle of the Have-Nots against the Haves has to pass through, they always and everywhere represent the interests of the Have-Nots as a whole.

The Activists, therefore, are on the one hand, practically, the most advanced and resolute section of the Have-Nots movements of every country, that section which pushes forward all others; on the other hand, theoretically, they have over the great mass of the Have-Nots the advantage of clearly understanding the line of march, the conditions, and the ultimate general results of the Have-Nots movement.

The immediate aim of the Activists is the same as that of all other Have-Not parties: formation of the Have-Nots into a united movement, overthrow of the Haves supremacy, conquest of political, economic, and social power by the Have-Nots.

The theoretical conclusions of the Activists are in no way based on ideas or principles that have been invented, or discovered, by this or that would-be universal reformer.

They merely express, in general terms, actual relations springing from an existing equality struggle, from a historical movement going on under our very eyes. The abolition of existing inequalities is not at all a distinctive feature of activism.

All inequalities in the past have continually been subject to historical change consequent upon the change in historical conditions.

Previous revolutions have been focused on labour interests and on the abolition of private property. The French Revolution, for example, abolished feudal property in favour of Haves property.

The distinguishing feature of Communism was not the abolition of property generally, but the abolition of Haves property. Indeed, the theory of the Communists may be summed up by the single sentence: Abolition of private property.

In contrast, the Activists recognize that a silo movement focused on the abolition of private property can, in turn, be co-opted by the Haves for their own benefit. State-held property also is subject to capture by the Haves. Indeed, the complete power of the Haves is the final and most complete expression of the system of producing and appropriating wealth and influence, deriving from the ruthless and cynical exploitation of the Have-Nots by the Haves.

The theory of the Activists may be summed up in the single sentence: Fight inequality and vested interests.

Activists have been reproached with the desire of abolishing the right of people to protect their vested interests, these interests being the preservation of the status quo, the preservation of continuity over change.

The right of people to equality! To their protection against vested interests! Do you mean the protected interests of the hard working Have-Not? There is no need to abolish that; the all-pervasive power of technology has relegated that to the scrapheap of history. The powerless, the well meaning individuals, all these Have-Nots are daily being co-opted for the wellbeing of the Haves.

But does preservation of vested interests create any benefit for the Have-Nots? Not a bit. It creates inequality, *i.e.*, that type of inequality that exhibits itself in the solidification and perpetuation of the power in the modern system; the type of power that allows the Haves to cloak the cynicism of self interest in the language of progress for all. Inequality, in its present form, is based on the antagonism of power and democratic rhetoric.

Let us examine both sides of this antagonism.

To have power is to have not only a purely personal quality, but a collective social *status* in society. Power is a collective product, and only by the united action of many members, nay, in the last resort, only by the united action of all members of society, can it be set in motion.

Power is therefore not only personal; it is a social asset.

When, therefore, power is converted into vested interests, into the interests of all members of society, personal interest is not thereby transferred away from the individual into a purely social asset. It is only the social purpose of the power that is changed. It loses its self-interested character.

Let us now take democratic rhetoric.

Rhetoric is the route to personal power, and democratic rhetoric the route to social power. What therefore the individual appropriates by means of their rhetoric becomes the foundation for their individual power and status. We by no means intend to abolish this personal appropriation of the products of their actions, the product of their own beliefs and interests. All that we want to do away with is the miserable character of this personal appropriation, under which the individual lives merely to increase their own self-interest, and is encouraged to the pursuit of this personal self-interest against the broader social interest of the society in which they live.

In the Haves society, personal power is but a means to increase and consolidate social power. In an Activist society, personal power is a means by which to increase the social welfare of society as a whole.

In a Haves society, therefore, the past dominates the present; in an Activist society, the present dominates the past. In a Haves society, power is independent and has individuality, while the living person is dependent and has no individuality.

And the abolition of this state of things is called by the Haves 'the abolition of individuality and freedom'! And rightly so! The abolition of Haves individuality, Haves independence, and Haves freedom is undoubtedly aimed at.

By freedom is meant, under the present Haves appropriation of the term, freedom to pursue narrow personal self-interest and the power to separate and divide those forces that seek to align themselves against these narrow vested interests.

But if narrow self-interest and the power associated with the Haves disappears, then so does the inequality associated with this narrow self-interest! The ability of the Haves to appropriate political, economic, and social power in pursuit of the perpetuation of their personal power disappears and opens the door to a progressive alliance of wider societal interests among the Have-Nots.

You are horrified at our intending to do away with individualism. But in your existing society, individualism is already done away with for nine-tenths of the population; its existence for the few is solely due to its non-existence in the hands of those nine-tenths. You reproach us, therefore, with intending to do away with a form of social power, the necessary condition for whose existence is the non-existence of any social power for the immense majority of society.

In one word, you reproach us with intending to do away with your personal power. Precisely so; that is just what we intend.

From the moment when personal power can no longer be converted into a social power capable of being monopolised, *i.e.*, from the moment when individual ideas or beliefs can no longer be transformed into the perpetuation of the power of the entrenched interests of the Haves, the limiting and regressive force that is individuality vanishes. What replaces it is the power of Activism.

You must, therefore, confess that by "individual" you mean no other person than the Haves, than the middle-class owner of social power. This person must, indeed, be swept out of the way, and made impossible.

Activism deprives no person of the power to appropriate the products of society; all that it does is to deprive them of the power to subjugate others by means of such appropriations.

It has been objected that upon the abolition of private power and self-interest, that all work will cease, and universal laziness will overtake us.

According to this, Haves society ought long ago to have gone to the dogs through sheer idleness; for those of its members who work, acquire nothing, and those who acquire anything do not work. The whole of this objection is but another expression of the tautology: that there can no longer be any motivation to acquire individual interests when there are no longer any individual interests.

All objections urged against the Activist mode of exercising political power, have, in the same way, been urged against the Activist mode of producing and appropriating ideas about power. But the Activist movement does not advocate eliminating power or interests, any more than it is about eliminating private property. The Activists embrace private property and the individual rewards to individual work. Instead, the objective of the Activist movement is to relocate power and interests, away from the unequal modern distribution in favour of a less vested and more equitable distribution. To the Haves, the disappearance of individual power might seem to be the disappearance of life itself, just as the disappearance of elite culture might seem equal to the disappearance of all culture.

That power and that culture, the loss of which one laments, are, for the enormous majority, a mere training to act as a machine.

But don't wrangle with us so long as you apply, to our intended abolition of Haves power and interests, the standard of your Haves notions of freedom, culture, law, etc. Your very ideas are but the outgrowth of the conditions of your unequal Haves culture, just as your jurisprudence is but the will of your class made into a law for all, a will whose essential character and direction are determined by the economical conditions of existence of your class.

The selfish misconception that induces you to transform into eternal laws of nature and of reason, the social forms springing from your present mode of allocating power and interests – historical relations that rise and disappear as inequality fluctuates – this misconception you share with every ruling class that has preceded you. What you see clearly in the case of ancient power, what you admit in the case of feudal power, you are of course forbidden to admit in the case of your own Haves form of power.

Some forms of activism, and indeed Communism, have argued against the traditional foundation on which the present family, the Haves family, is based. On capital, on private gain. In its completely developed form, these silos of activism proclaim, this family exists only among the Haves. But not every form of activism admits that this state of things finds its complement in the practical absence of the traditional family unit among the Have-Nots, and in public prostitution.

Instead, the Activist Party recognizes and celebrates the various incarnations of modern families and private social structures: the churches and synagogues along with the atheists; the working and non-working groups along with the gatherings of leisure and play; the sports or arts or spiritual clubs together with the addiction and recovery societies; and all of the cultural gatherings that nourish Have-Nots even in the presence of vast inequality. The powers enjoyed by Haves families in modern society will vanish as a matter of course when their complement arrives, but the families of the ex-Haves nevertheless can survive, even in a world of declining inequality.

Do you charge us with wanting to stop the exploitation of children by their parents? To this crime we plead guilty, as did the Communists and other groups of activists over time.

But, instead of obliterating the most hallowed of relations, we advocate supplementing home education, not destroying it. Both Haves and Have-Nots can benefit from all categories of education. Haves are not the only members of society with permission to access the greatest schools and universities, nor should they have any preference in such admission.

Our education! Is not that also social, and determined by the social conditions under which we educate, by the intervention direct or indirect, of society, by means of schools, etc.? The Activists have not invented the intervention of society in education; they do but seek to alter the character of that intervention, and to rescue education from the influence of the Haves.

And what about the inequalities of gender, race, ethnicity, sexual preferences, and other minority conditions? A century ago, many Haves saw women as mere instruments of production. African-Americans were slaves when the early incarnations of Communism arose. Not only in the past, but also in the present, too many Haves see the weaker or less powerful members of society as opportunities for exploitation.

The Activist has no patience for such views, whether among Haves or Have-Nots, or among Communists or Capitalists. For the Activist, reducing inequality is a moral imperative. The modern view embraces all human beings, Haves and Have-Nots, regardless of gender, race, or sexual preference. Haves are the target of the activism because of their power and their vested interests, not because they occupy a particular status.

Haves marriage was, in the past, a system of wives in common and thus, at the most, what the Activists might possibly be reproached with is that they desire to introduce, in substitution for a hypocritically concealed, an openly legalised community of women. Consistent with their views of power and vested interests generally, the Activists embrace freedom and free choice with respect to marriage, reproduction, and sex, and oppose the subjugation of the powerless.

Some activists desire to abolish countries and nationality. As that argument goes, since the Have-Nots must first of all acquire political supremacy, must rise to be the leading class of the nation, must constitute itself *the* nation, it is so far, itself national, though not in the Haves sense of the word.

National differences and antagonism between peoples are daily more and more pronounced, owing to the development of the Haves, to freedom of commerce, to the world market, to inequalities in technology, economic and intellectual property rights, natural resources and in the conditions of life corresponding thereto.

The supremacy of the Have-Nots will cause them to vanish still faster. United action, of the leading civilised countries at least, is one of the first conditions for the emancipation of the Have-Nots.

In proportion as the exploitation of one individual by another will also be put an end to, the exploitation of one nation by another will also be put an end to. In proportion as the antagonism between classes within the nation vanishes, the hostility of one nation to another will come to an end.

As to religion, the Activists do not advocate any particular view. Does it require deep intuition to comprehend that human ideas, views, and conception, in one word, human consciousness, changes with every change in the conditions of material existence, in social relations and in social life?

What else does the history of ideas prove, than that intellectual production changes its character in proportion as material production is changed? The ruling ideas of each age have ever been the ideas of its ruling class.

When people speak of the ideas that revolutionise society, they do but express that fact that within the old society the elements of a new one have been created, and that the dissolution of the old ideas keeps even pace with the dissolution of the old conditions of existence.

When the ancient world was in its last throes, the ancient religions were overcome by Christianity. When Christian ideas succumbed in the 18th century to rationalist ideas, feudal society fought its death battle with the then-revolutionary Haves. The ideas of religious liberty and freedom of conscience merely gave expression to the sway of free competition within the domain of knowledge.

"Undoubtedly," it will be said, "religious, moral, philosophical, and juridical ideas have been modified in the course of historical development. But religion, morality, philosophy, political science, and law, constantly survived this change."

"There are, besides, eternal truths, such as Freedom, Justice, etc., that are common to all states of society. But united Activism would abolish eternal truths, challenge all religion, and all morality, sometimes even constituting them on a new basis; it therefore would act in contradiction to all past historical experience."

What does this accusation reduce itself to? The history of all past society has consisted in the development of class antagonisms, antagonisms that assumed different forms at different epochs.

But whatever form they may have taken, one fact is common to all past ages, *viz.*, the exploitation of one part of society by the other. No wonder, then, that the social consciousness of past ages, despite all the multiplicity and variety it displays, moves within certain common forms, or general ideas, which cannot completely vanish except with the total disappearance of class antagonisms.

The Activist revolution is the most radical rupture with traditional relations; no wonder that its development involved the most radical rupture with traditional ideas. Activism recognizes the insights with respect to the past role of religions in society, but comes to a different conclusion. Instead of fighting against a particular religion or religious view, or against all religions, Activists embrace diverse approaches to religion, as with other views. The primary focus of the Activists in this area, as in all areas, is the attack against inequality and its view of religious approaches is consistent with that focus.

But let us have done with the Haves' objections to Activism.

We have seen above, that the first step in the revolution by the working class is to raise the Have-Nots to the position of ruling class to win the battle of democracy.

The Have-Nots will use their political supremacy to wrest, by degree, substantial degrees of power and vested interests from the Haves, not to centralise all instruments of production in the hands of the State, *i.e.*, of the Have-Nots organised as the ruling class, but to recalibrate power and interests so as to create a more equal society.

Of course, in the beginning, this cannot be effected except by means of incremental change; by means of measures, therefore, which appear economically insufficient and untenable, but which, in the course of the movement, build on themselves, necessitate further inroads upon the old social order, and are unavoidable as a means of entirely revolutionising the concentration of power.

Some groups seeking such ends will label themselves activists, though the change they seek is dangerous and oppressive. There are the terrorists, the white supremacists and neo-Nazis, the thugs and bullies who advocate violence and genocide, the supposed zealots who misappropriate religions and creeds for vicious ends. These groups are activists in name only, and will not find support under a united Activist umbrella. The true Activists embrace basic measures that are meant to improve the quality of human lives without violence and oppression. Individual Activists and groups will, of course, prefer one particular agenda over another. But all Activists should embrace certain minimal measures and act together to further those measures. They can be regarded as a minimal baseline, to be amplified, but not abandoned.

These measures will, of course, be different in different countries.

Nevertheless, in most advanced countries, the following will be pretty generally applicable.

1. Guarantee a minimal acceptable standard of living and meaningful opportunities for work.
2. Preserve the environment and the interests of future generations.
3. Respect diversity, including gender, race, ethnicity, and sexual preferences.
4. Supply access to affordable health care.
5. Facilitate education, knowledge creation, and free expression.
6. Root out and pursue corruption and the entrenchment of power, both in government and in the private sector.
7. Provide security and protect private property, including intellectual property.
8. Enable access to modern technology, including high-speed connectivity.
9. Create incentives for a financial system that facilitates real economic growth and productivity.
10. Empower the locality over the state.

When, in the course of development, class distinctions have disappeared, and inequality has been reduced, the public power will lose its political character. Political power, properly so called, is merely the organised power of one class for oppressing another. If the Have-Nots during their contest with the Haves are compelled, by the force of circumstances, to organise itself as a class, if, by means of a revolution, they make themselves the ruling class, and, as such, sweep away by force the old conditions of power and vested interests, then they will, along with these conditions, have swept away the conditions for the existence of class antagonisms and of classes generally, and will thereby have abolished their own supremacy as a class. The Activists are, above all, cognizant that the Have-Nots take precautions to avoid transformation in their own version of hegemony.

In place of the old Haves society, with its classes and class antagonisms, we shall have an association, in which the free development of each is the condition for the free development of all.

# III. Socialist vs. Activist in Practice

## 1. Sectoral Activism

### A: Financial Activism

Owing to their historical position, it became the vocation of the aristocracies of underperforming corporate managers to write pamphlets against modern shareholder activists. In the shareholder spring of 2012, and in proxy reform agitation, these corporate aristocracies again succumbed to the hateful upstart. Thenceforth, a serious financial and governance struggle was altogether out of the question. A literary battle through the media alone remained possible. But even in the domain of literature the old cries of the pre-activist period had become impossible.

The early activists might justifiably have been derided as lazy, simply picking the low-hanging fruit of inefficient corporate conglomerates. But the subsequent activists were more sophisticated: they used financial analyses and in-depth operational insights to pick their targets and force change. These strategies benefited those Have-Nots whose pensions were tied up in the activists' targets, even as they threatened the jobs of the aristocratic managers (and also, ironically, of many of the Have-Nots).

In order to arouse sympathy, the corporate aristocracy was obliged to lose sight, apparently, of its own interests, and to formulate their indictment against the shareholder activists in the interest of the exploited employees and purported long-term interests of their corporations. Thus, the aristocracy took their revenge by singing lampoons on their new masters and whispering in their ears sinister prophesies of coming catastrophe.

In this way arose financial activism: half lamentation, half lampoon; half an echo of the past, half menace of the future; at times, by its bitter, witty and incisive criticism, striking the corporate manager to the very heart's core; but always ludicrous in its effect, through total incapacity to comprehend the march of modern history.

The corporate aristocracy, in order to rally the people to them, waved the Have Not alms-bag in front for a banner. But the people, so often as it joined them, saw on their hindquarters the old feudal coats of arms, and deserted with loud and irreverent laughter.

In pointing out that their mode of exploitation was different to that of the Haves, the corporate managers forget that they exploited under circumstances and conditions that were quite different and that are now antiquated. In showing that, under their rule, the modern Have-Nots never existed, they forget that the modern Haves are the necessary offspring of their own form of society.

For the rest, so little do they conceal the reactionary character of their criticism that their chief accusation against the Haves amounts to this, that under the Haves régime a class is being developed which is destined to cut up root and branch the old order of society.

What they upbraid the Haves with is not so much that it creates Have-Nots as that it creates revolutionary Have-Nots.

In political practice, therefore, they join in all coercive measures against the employee class; and in ordinary life, despite their high-falutin phrases, they stoop to pick up the golden apples dropped from the tree of industry, and to barter truth, love, and honour, for traffic in branded clothing, processed foods, payday loans, and quick stimulants.

Financial activism succeeds only within its silo. It is the singular focus on profit that is the most potentially socially damaging aspect of financial activists' self-interested approaches. Shareholders gain from share prices increasing, to be sure. But what if those shareholder gains are at the expense of society's welfare overall? What about the company's employees? Or lenders? Or the environment? Or consumers? Again, it is the Haves over the Have-Nots. These costs are real and well known: economists have long understood how "externalities" can arise from the relentless pursuit of profit. Even the leading advocates of shareholder wealth maximization have softened, recognizing that gains to shareholders are not justified when they come at the expense of other corporate constituents.

Financial activism is profoundly selfish. It is not cognizant of whether other wealth is being destroyed. It lacks a social or moral compass. It is, ultimately and necessarily, a self-interested pursuit. To the extent financial activism aligns with the interests of non-shareholders, it is a happy accident, not a strategy. Because of these limitations, financial activism ultimately lacks the capacity of revolution. It cannot and will not achieve political force on its own.

## B: Environmental Activism

Shareholder activists are not the only class under attack from the Haves, not the only class whose conditions of existence pined and perished in the atmosphere of modern Haves society. The medieval polluters and the small peasant proprietors were the precursors of the modern pillager Haves. In those countries which are but little developed, industrially and commercially, these two classes still vegetate side by side with the rising Haves.

In countries where modern civilisation has become fully developed, a new class of toxic Haves has been formed, ever renewing itself as miners, frackers, pipeline-builders, and producers of carbon and waste. The individual members of this class, however, are being constantly hurled down into the Have Nots by the action of competition, and, as modern industry develops, they even see the moment approaching when they will completely disappear as an independent section of modern society, to be replaced in manufactures, agriculture and commerce, by overlookers, bailiffs, and shopmen.

In countries like China and India, where the peasants constitute far more than half of the population, it was natural that writers who sided with the Have-Nots against the Haves should use, in their criticism of the ruling régime, the standard of the peasant, and from the standpoint of these intermediate classes, should take up the cudgels for low-level employees, those assemblers of mobile phones for pennies a day. Thus arose petty-Haves environmentalism.

This school of environmentalism dissected with great acuteness the contradictions in the conditions of modern production. It laid bare the hypocritical apologies of economists relating to externalities. It proved, incontrovertibly, the disastrous side-effects of machinery and division of labour; the concentration of capital and land in a few privileged hands whose single focus ignores anything other than the illusory lure of efficient markets; overproduction and crises; it pointed out the inevitable ruin of the petty Haves and peasant, the misery of the Have-Nots, the anarchy in production, the crying inequalities in the distribution of wealth, the industrial war of extermination between nations, the dissolution of old moral bonds, of the old family relations, of the old nationalities.

In its positive aims, however, this form of environmentalism aspires either to restoring the balance between efficiency and social responsibility, and with them the old economic relations, or to cramping the modern means of production and of exchange within the framework of the old economic relations that have been, and were bound to be, exploded by those means. In either case, it is both reactionary and Utopian. Its last words are: the Roundtable for Sustainable Palm Oil, Swampy, Earth Day, Greenham Common, and composting.

Its last words are hollow, simply attacking on the grounds of corporate guilt and patriarchal relations. The different types of environmental activists are each in their own silo, apart from the financial activists, and apart from the connections to political power that might sustain their longer-term success.

Ultimately, when stubborn historical facts had dispersed all intoxicating effects of self-deception, this form of environmentalism ended in a miserable fit of the blues.

## C: Local Political Activism

The grass roots global political movements, which originated under the pressure of the Haves in power, and which were expressions of the struggle against this power, were introduced into Tunisia and Egypt and later the United States and Europe at a time when the Haves, in those countries, had just begun their contest with activism.

Western philosophers, would be philosophers, and beaux esprits (men of letters), eagerly seized on these movements, only forgetting that, when they emerged, other categories of activists had not immigrated along with them.

The work of those tweeting about the Arab Spring, Brexit, or Trump consisted solely in bringing the new political activist ideas into harmony with their ancient philosophical conscience, or rather, in annexing the political activist ideas without deserting their own philosophic point of view.

This annexation took place in the same way in which a foreign language is appropriated, namely, by translation.

It is well known how the monks wrote silly lives of Catholic Saints over the manuscripts on which the classical works of ancient heathendom had been written. The early political activists reversed this process with their profane expropriation of political rhetoric. They wrote their philosophical nonsense beneath the original. For instance, beneath the criticism of Hillary Clinton, they wrote about the need to dethrone the ruling Clinton dynasty, and beneath the criticism of British membership in the European Union, they wrote about the alienation of sovereignty, and so forth.

The introduction of these philosophical phrases at the back of the historical criticisms, they dubbed "Power to the People," "The Democratic Will," "Internationalism," "Make America Great Again," and so on.

The activist claims were thus completely emasculated. And, since it ceased in the hands of the activists to express the struggle of one class with the other, they felt conscious of having overcome "one-sidedness" and of representing, not true requirements, but the requirements of Truth; not the interests of the Have-Nots, but the interests of Human Nature, of Humans in general, who belongs to no class, has no reality, who exists only in the misty realm of philosophical fantasy.

Too many political activists, who took their schoolchild task so seriously and solemnly, and extolled its poor stock-in-trade in such a mountebank fashion, meanwhile gradually lost their pedantic innocence. The fight against the aristocracy, and even absolute monarchy, in other words, the liberal movement, became more earnest. By this, the long-wished opportunity was offered to "True" activists of confronting the political movement with their demands, of hurling the traditional anathemas against liberalism, against representative government, against competition, freedom of the press, legislation, liberty and equality, and of preaching to the masses that they had nothing to gain, and everything to lose, by these movements.

To the absolute governments, with their following of parsons, professors, country squires, and officials, it served as a welcome scarecrow against the threatening new Haves.

It was a sweet finish, after the bitter pills of flogging, bullets, and tear gas with which these same governments, just at that time, dosed the various risings.

While this "True" activism thus served the government as a weapon for fighting the Haves, it, at the same time, directly represented a reactionary interest, the interest of Philistines. The petty-Haves class, a relic of the sixteenth century, and since then constantly cropping up again under the various forms, is the real social basis of the existing state of things.

The political activists who took to the streets in the Arab Spring and other movements were brave, passionate, committed people, fighting for just causes and determined to use the power of their democratic presence. But Activism without defence against centralised power further begets centralised power. In too many nations, governments deflect political activism as self interested, corrupt, or the arm of some destabilising force. Control of the media, backed up by brutal police and security forces are their weapons. And political activists compete again, within their own country, fighting for different visions of reform, the outcome at best futile, at worst murderous.

Local community activists are more practical, less revolutionary. They target the issues close by – speeding motorbikes, fly-tippers dumping rubbish, dangerous playgrounds. These causes are as noble as the grand aims and ambitions of those who seek to change a country or the planet. Only the truly and persistently local can withstand the magnet of the centralised Haves class.

To preserve this class is to preserve the existing state of things. The industrial and political supremacy of the Haves threatens it with certain destruction – on the one hand, from the concentration of capital; on the other, from the rise of revolutionary Have-Nots. "True" activism appeared to kill these two birds with one stone. It spread like an epidemic.

The robe of speculative cobwebs, embroidered with flowers of rhetoric, steeped in the dew of sickly sentiment, this transcendental robe in which some activists wrapped their sorry "eternal truths", all skin and bone, served to wonderfully increase the spread of their ideas amongst such a public.

And on its part the centralized, federal powers recognised, more and more, their own calling as the bombastic representative of the petty-Have Philistine.

It proclaimed the centralized nation to be the model nation, and the petty Philistine to be the typical man. To every villainous meanness of this model man, it gave a hidden, higher, somehow activist interpretation, the exact contrary of its real character. It went to the extreme length of directly opposing the "brutally destructive" tendency of activism, and of proclaiming its supreme and impartial contempt of all class struggles. With very few exceptions, all the so-called activist publications and posts that now circulate in the world belong to the domain of this foul and enervating literature.

# 2. Thematic Activism

A part of the Haves philosophy is desirous of redressing social grievances in order to secure the continued existence of Haves society.

To this section belong economists, philanthropists, humanitarians, improvers of the condition of the working class, organisers of charity, members of societies for the prevention of cruelty to animals, temperance fanatics, hole-and-corner reformers of every imaginable kind. This form of activism has, moreover, been worked out into complete systems.

The activist haves want all the advantages of modern social conditions without the struggles and dangers necessarily resulting therefrom. They desire the existing state of society, minus its revolutionary and disintegrating elements. They wish for Haves without Have-Nots. They naturally conceive the world in which it is supreme to be the best; and activism develops this comfortable conception into various more or less complete systems. In requiring the Have-Nots to carry out such a system, and thereby to march straightway into the social New Jerusalem, it but requires in reality, that the Have-Nots should remain within the bounds of existing society, but should cast away all its hateful ideas concerning the Haves.

A second, and more practical, but less systematic, form of this activism sought to depreciate every revolutionary movement in the eyes of the working class by showing that no mere political reform, but only a change in the material conditions of existence, in economical relations, could be of any advantage to them. By changes in the material conditions of existence, this form of activism, however, by no means understands abolition of the Haves' relations of production, an abolition that can be affected only by a revolution, but administrative reforms, based on the continued existence of these relations; reforms, therefore, that in no respect affect the relations between Haves and Have-Nots, but, at the best, lessen the cost, and simplify the administrative work, of Haves government.

In thematic terms, activism can be grouped into themes as positive, negative and nihilistic. Positive activism is inherently attractive. It seeks positive changes and outcomes. Its theme is affirmative, and active. In contrast, negative activism is inherently oppositional. It leverages mistrust and suspicion. The rise in nationalism is negative, driven by the urge to topple governments, the primal force to oppose the other.

Other activism is neither positive nor negative, but nihilistic. It destroys all, rubble and ashes, with the goal of tearing down the slow moving institutions of state, the privileged political classes, the greedy corporations, and the self-interested politicians whose individualistic focus on their own self-interest both perpetuates social inertia and incentivizes grassroots movements.

Activism attains adequate expression for the Haves when, and only when, it becomes a mere figure of speech, purporting to weigh in favor of the Have-Nots. Free trade: for the benefit of the Have-Nots. Protective duties: for the benefit of the Have-Nots. Prison Reform: for the benefit of the Have-Nots. This is the last word and the only seriously meant word of Haves activism.

It is summed up in the phrase: the Have is a Have—for the benefit of the Have-Not.

# 3. Critical-Utopian Activism

We do not here refer to that literature which, in every great modern revolution, has always given voice to the demands of the Have-Nots such as the writings of Babeuf, Ehrenreich, Piketty and others. The first direct attempts of the Have-Nots to attain its own ends, made in times of universal excitement, when feudal society was being overthrown, necessarily failed, owing to the then undeveloped state of the Have-Nots, as well as to the absence of the economic conditions for its emancipation, conditions that had yet to be produced, and could be produced by the impending Haves epoch alone. The revolutionary literature that accompanied these first movements of the Have-Nots had necessarily a reactionary character. It inculcated universal asceticism and social levelling in its crudest form.

The various activist approaches and systems, properly so called, spring into existence in the early undeveloped period, described above, of the struggle between Have-Not and Have. The founders of these systems see, indeed, the class antagonisms, as well as the action of the decomposing elements in the prevailing form of society. But the Have-Not, as yet in its infancy, offers to them the spectacle of a class without any historical initiative or any independent political movement. Since the development of class antagonism keeps even pace with the development of industry, the economic situation, as they find it, does not as yet offer to them the material conditions for the emancipation of the Have-Not. They therefore search after a new social science, after new social laws, that are to create these conditions.

Historical action is to yield to their personal inventive action; historically created conditions of emancipation to fantastic ones; and the gradual, spontaneous class organisation of the Have-Nots to an organisation of society especially contrived by these inventors. Future history resolves itself, in their eyes, into the propaganda and the practical carrying out of their social plans. In the formation of their plans, they are conscious of caring chiefly for the interests of the Have-Nots, as being the most suffering class. Only from the point of view of being the most suffering class do the Have-Nots exist for them. The undeveloped state of the class struggle, as well as their own surroundings, causes Activists of this kind to consider themselves far superior to other antagonisms. They want to improve the condition of every member of society, even that of the most favoured. Hence, they habitually appeal to society at large, without distinction; nay, by preference, to the wealthy and powerful. For how can people, when once they understand their system, fail to see in it the best possible plan of the best possible state of society? Hence, they reject all political, and especially all revolutionary action; they wish to attain their ends by peaceful means, necessarily doomed to failure, and by the force of example, to pave the way for the new social Gospel. Such fantastic pictures of future society, painted at a time when the Have Not is still in a very undeveloped state and has but a fantastic conception of its own position, correspond with the first instinctive yearnings for a general reconstruction of society.

But these Activist ideas contain also a critical element. They attack every principle of existing society. Hence, they are full of the most valuable materials for the enlightenment of the Have Nots. The practical measures proposed in them – such as the pitching of tents by Occupy Wall Street, the use of social media in Tahrir Square, the bloodied fake furs of the animal movements – all these proposals point solely to the disappearance of antagonisms which were, at that time, only just cropping up, and which, in these publications, are recognised in their earliest indistinct and undefined forms only. These proposals, therefore, are of a purely Utopian character.

The significance of Critical-Utopian Activism bears an inverse relation to historical development. In proportion as the modern struggle develops and takes definite shape, this fantastic standing apart from the contest, these fantastic attacks on it, lose all practical value and all theoretical justification. Therefore, although the originators of these systems were, in many respects, revolutionary, their disciples have, in every case, formed mere reactionary sects. They hold fast by the original views of their masters, in opposition to the progressive historical development of the Have-Nots. They, therefore, endeavour, and that consistently, to deaden the struggle and to reconcile the varied antagonisms. They still dream of experimental realisation of their social Utopias, of founding isolated "phalansteres", of establishing "Home Colonies" or Interplanetary Settlements, "Little Icarias" or Biospheres – duodecimo editions of the New Jerusalem – and to realise all these castles in the air, they are compelled to appeal to the feelings and purses of the Haves. By degrees, they sink into the category of the reactionary or conservative activists depicted above, differing from these only by more systematic pedantry, and by their fanatical and superstitious belief in the miraculous effects of their social science.

They, therefore, violently oppose all political action on the part of the Have-Nots; such action, according to them, can only result from blind unbelief in the new Gospel. The parties with political power on every continent, in many countries, including those who seemed to have risen to power with the support of one silo activist movement, now come to oppose the activists in aggregate.

# IV. Position of the Activists in Relation to the Various Existing Opposition Parties

Section II has made clear the relations of the Activists to the existing Have-Nots, in England, America, and throughout the world.

The Activists fight for the attainment of the immediate aims, for the enforcement of the momentary interests of the Have-Nots; but in the movement of the present, they also represent and take care of the future of that movement. In many places, the Activists ally with particular political parties and other movements, sometimes against the conservative and radical Haves, reserving, however, the right to take up a critical position in regard to phases and illusions traditionally handed down from the great Revolution.

They fight in many countries, but they never cease, for a single instant, to instil the clearest possible recognition of the hostile antagonism between Haves and Have-Nots, in order that Have-Nots may straightway use, as so many weapons against the Haves, the social and political conditions that the Haves must necessarily introduce along with its supremacy, and in order that, after the fall of the reactionary classes, the fight against the Haves itself may immediately begin.

The Activists turn their attention chiefly to West, because countries are on the eve of a Have-Nots revolution that is bound to be carried out under more advanced conditions of civilisation and with a much more developed Have-Not sector than that of the industrial revolution of the nineteenth century, the conglomerate era of the twentieth century, and because the Haves revolution today will be but the prelude to an immediately following Have-Not revolution.

In short, the Activists everywhere support every revolutionary movement against the existing social and political order of things. In all these movements, they bring to the front, as the leading question in each, the various questions set forth above, no matter what its degree of development at the time. Finally, they labour everywhere for the union and agreement of the activist movements of all countries.

The Activists disdain to conceal their views and aims. They openly declare that their ends can be attained only by the forcible overthrow of all existing social conditions. Let the Haves tremble at an Activist revolution. The Have-Nots have nothing to lose but their chains. They have a world to win.

**Activists of All Countries, Unite!**

# About the Authors

**Rupert Younger**

Rupert is co-founder and global managing partner of Finsbury, and founder director of Oxford University's Centre for Corporate Reputation. He is also co-author of *The Reputation Game*, a bestselling book published in 2017 drawing on his research at Oxford with case study examples from business, politics, the arts and wider society.

He is a regular commentator on how reputations are created, sustained, destroyed and rebuilt. His work and views are regularly featured in major news outlets including the BBC, CNN, the Financial Times, The Wall Street Journal, and the Times of London. He has a particular expertise in global issues advocacy and has led successful reputation and communications engagement campaigns for global organisations over the past twenty-five years. He has worked for and against financial activists, and has studied – and also worked on – broader societal activism campaigns in his dual roles at Oxford and Finsbury.

Rupert chaired The University of Oxford's Socially Responsible Investment Committee of Council (2011-2017) and is a member of the Senior Common Rooms at Worcester College, Oxford and St Antony's College, Oxford. He is a Trustee of the international mine clearance and humanitarian charity The HALO Trust, and was appointed by HM Queen Elizabeth II as her High Sheriff of Hampshire for 2013-14. He is also a member of the Royal Company of Archers, the Queen's Bodyguard in Scotland, and is the bass player/songwriter for an indie rock band called Chalk Flowers.


**Frank Partnoy**

Frank will be joining UC Berkeley as a tenured law professor in summer 2018. He is currently the George E. Barrett Professor of Law and Finance and the founding director of the Center for Corporate and Securities Law at the University of San Diego. He is a graduate of Yale Law School, and has degrees in mathematics and economics from the University of Kansas.

After law school, he clerked for the Honorable Michael B. Mukasey, in the Southern District of New York, and then worked as a derivatives structurer at Morgan Stanley and CS First Boston during the mid-1990s. He wrote F.I.A.S.C.O.: Blood in the Water on Wall Street, a best-selling book about his experiences there. He subsequently worked at Covington & Burling, in Washington, D.C., but he didn't write a book about that.

Since 1997, he has been a law professor at the University of San Diego. He has written more than two dozen scholarly articles published in academic journals including The University of Chicago Law Review, The University of Pennsylvania Law Review, and The Journal of Finance. He also is the co-author of a leading corporate law casebook.

His recent trade press books include *WAIT: The Art and Science of Delay*, *Infectious Greed: How Deceit and Risk Corrupted the Financial Markets*, and *The Match King: Ivar Kreuger, The Financial Genius Behind a Century of Wall Street Scandals*, which was a finalist for the Financial Times/Goldman Sachs Business Book of the Year in 2009.

He has written regularly for The New York Times and the Financial Times, as well as The New York Review of Books and The Atlantic. He has appeared on numerous media programs, including 60 Minutes, The NewsHour, and The Daily Show with Jon Stewart. He also has testified as an expert before both houses of Congress, and has been a consultant to many major corporations, banks, pension funds, and hedge funds regarding various aspects of financial markets and regulation.

28158984R00022

Printed in Great Britain
by Amazon